MW01002937

A DORLING KINDERSLEY BOOK

First American Edition, 1992
10 9 8 7 6 5 4 3 2 1
Published in the United States by Dorling Kindersley, Inc.,
232 Madison Avenue, New York, New York 10016

For Sam

ISBN 1-56458-104-7
Library of Congress Catalog Card Number 92-52800

Color reproduction by Dot Gradations
Printed in Singapore by Tien Wah Press Ltd

Feathery
ANIMALS

Illustrated by
Kenneth Lilly

Written by
Angela Wilkes

DORLING KINDERSLEY, INC.
NEW YORK

Contents

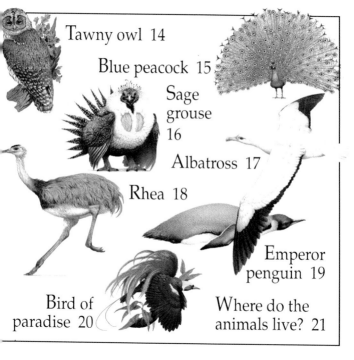

Painted bunting
The painted bunting uses its strong beak to crack open tough seeds.

Bald eagle
This eagle seizes
fish and small
animals in its long,
curved claws.

9

Roseate spoonbill
This wader uses its
spoon-shaped
bill to dig around
for shellfish in
muddy swamps.

10

Hoatzin
This bird can hardly fly. It uses its large wings to balance as it climbs trees.

11

Brown kiwi
This flightless
bird is covered
in long feathers
that look like
shaggy fur.

12

Ruby topaz hummingbird
The hummingbird hovers
in midair and sips flower
nectar with its long bill.

13

Tawny owl
This nighttime
hunter can
fly silently
because of its
soft, fringed
wing feathers.

14

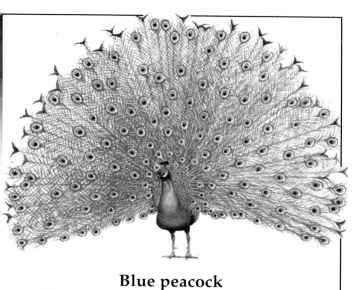

Blue peacock
The male bird fans out his elegant,
long tail feathers to attract a mate.

15

Sage grouse
The male sage grouse puffs out his chest feathers to make himself look big and important.

16

Albatross
This bird has the largest wing-span of any bird on Earth. It can glide for hours over the sea.

17

Rhea
This huge bird cannot fly,
but it can run very fast.

18

Emperor penguin
The emperor penguin swims very fast
in search of fish to eat, but it
cannot fly at all.

Bird of paradise
The male birds perform dances to show
off their feathers to female birds.

20

Where do the animals live?

Painted bunting
The Everglades,
North America

Bald eagle
North American
forests

Roseate spoonbill
The Everglades,
North America

Hoatzin
Amazon rain forests

Brown kiwi
New Zealand

**Ruby topaz
hummingbird**
Amazon rain forests

Tawny owl
European woodlands

Blue peacock
Southeast Asia

Sage grouse
North American
forests

Albatross
Antarctica

Rhea
The Pampas, South
America

Emperor penguin
Antarctica

Bird of paradise
Australasian
rain forests

21

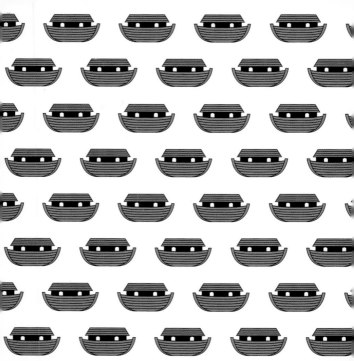